GAO

Report to the Chairman, Committee on Commerce, House of Representatives

I0410943

July 2000

INFORMATION SECURITY

Fundamental Weaknesses Place EPA Data and Operations at Risk

G A O

Accountability ★ Integrity ★ Reliability

GAO/AIMD-00-215

Contents

Abbreviations

EPA	Environmental Protection Agency
IG	Inspector General
NIST	National Institute of Standards and Technology
OEI	Office of Environmental Information
OMB	Office of Management and Budget

B-285625

July 6, 2000

The Honorable Tom Bliley
Chairman
Committee on Commerce
House of Representatives

Dear Mr. Chairman:

This report responds to your August 18, 1999, request that we evaluate the Environmental Protection Agency's (EPA) information security program. It expands on our February 17, 2000, statement, which provided our initial findings;[1] discusses EPA's actions since mid-February to address the weaknesses we identified; and recommends needed corrective actions. On June 16, 2000, we issued a "Limited Official Use" report to you that detailed specific technical weaknesses found during our tests. Due to their sensitivity, those details are not included in this version of the report for public release.

In 1997 and again in 1999, EPA's Inspector General (IG) reported serious inadequacies in the agency's information security planning, control of Internet services, and monitoring of network activities as well as an absence of formal firewall technologies to protect EPA from outside intruders.[2] Your request for our evaluation was based largely on your concerns about EPA's progress in addressing these problems. Specifically, you asked that we (1) evaluate EPA's computer-based controls, (2) determine the extent and impact of computer security incidents at EPA, and (3) evaluate the agency's information security program management. Our objectives, scope, and methodology are discussed in more detail in appendix I. We performed our work in accordance with generally accepted government auditing standards.

---

[1] *Information Security: Fundamental Weaknesses Place EPA Data and Operations at Risk* (GAO/T-AIMD-00-97, February 17, 2000).

[2] *EPA's Internet Connectivity Controls,* Office of Inspector General Report of Audit (Redacted Version), September, 5, 1997, and *Audit of EPA's Fiscal 1998 Financial Statements,* Office of Inspector General Audit Report Number 99B0003, September 28, 1999.

Results in Brief

Our review found serious and pervasive problems that essentially rendered EPA's agencywide information security program ineffective. Our tests of computer-based controls concluded that the computer operating systems and the agencywide computer network that support most of EPA's mission-related and financial operations were riddled with security weaknesses. Of particular concern is that many of the most serious weaknesses we identified—those related to inadequate protection from intrusions via the Internet and poor security planning—had been previously reported to EPA management in 1997 by EPA's IG.

The negative effects of such weaknesses are illustrated by EPA's own records, which show several serious computer security incidents since early 1998 that have resulted in damage and disruption to agency operations. In addition, we identified deficiencies in EPA's incident detection and handling capabilities that limited EPA's ability to fully understand or assess the nature of or damage due to intrusions into and misuse of its computer systems. As a result of these weaknesses, EPA's computer systems and the operations that rely on these systems were highly vulnerable to tampering, disruption, and misuse from both internal and external sources. Moreover, EPA could not ensure the protection of sensitive business and financial data maintained on its larger computer systems or supported by its agencywide network.

Since the close of our audit in mid-February, EPA has moved aggressively to reduce the exposure of its systems and data and to correct the weaknesses we identified. These efforts, which include both short-term and long-term improvements to system access controls, are still underway, and we have not tested their effectiveness. However, EPA's actions show that the agency is taking a comprehensive and systematic approach that should help ensure that its efforts are effective.

Sustaining these improvements in today's dynamic computing environment will require continuing vigilance and management attention. Our review of EPA security program planning and management found that EPA's existing practices were largely a paper exercise that had done little to substantively identify, evaluate, and mitigate risks to the agency's data and systems. Accordingly, ensuring that corrective actions are effective on a continuing basis and that new risks are promptly identified and addressed will entail implementing significant improvements in the way EPA plans for and manages its information security program. In January 2000, EPA's Principal Deputy Assistant Administrator for the Office of Environmental

Information (OEI) issued a memorandum outlining planned improvements in the way EPA centrally manages its information security program. These planned management improvements, if effectively implemented, will begin to address many of the deficiencies we identified. However, implementing them will require a major adjustment in the way EPA's program and technical staff manage the agency's information security risks.

We are recommending that the EPA Administrator take a number of steps to strengthen access controls associated with EPA's major computer operating systems and agencywide network, enhance incident management efforts, and improve security program management and planning. In comments to a draft of this report, EPA concurred with our recommendations and described related corrective actions.

National Concern About Information Security Is Growing

Information security is an important consideration for any organization that depends on information systems and computer networks to carry out its mission or business. Computer security risks are significant, and they are growing. The dramatic expansion in computer interconnectivity and the exponential increase in the use of the Internet are changing the way our government, the nation, and much of the world communicate and conduct business. However, without proper safeguards, these developments pose enormous risks that make it easier for individuals and groups with malicious intentions to intrude into inadequately protected systems and use such access to obtain sensitive information, commit fraud, disrupt operations, or launch attacks against other organizations' sites. Further, the number of individuals with computer skills is increasing, and intrusion, or "hacking," techniques are readily available and relatively easy to use. The rash of cyber attacks launched in February 2000 against major Internet firms are illustrative of the risks associated with this new electronic age.

Computer-supported federal operations are also at risk. Our previous reports, and those of agency IGs, describe persistent computer security weaknesses that place a variety of critical federal operations at risk of disruption, fraud, and inappropriate disclosures.[3] This body of audit evidence led us, in 1997 and again in 1999, to designate computer security as a governmentwide high-risk area in reports to the Congress.[4] Our most recent summary analysis found that significant computer security weaknesses had been identified in 22 of the largest federal agencies, including EPA.[5]

How well federal agencies are addressing these risks is a topic of increasing interest in both the Congress and the executive branch. This is evidenced by recent hearings on information security, proposed legislation intended to strengthen information security, and the President's January 2000 *National Plan for Information Systems Protection*.[6] As outlined in this plan, a number of new, centrally managed entities have been established and projects have been initiated to assist agencies in strengthening their security programs and improving federal intrusion detection capabilities. In addition, on March 3, 2000, in response to recent Internet disruptions, the President issued a memorandum to the heads of executive departments and agencies urging them to renew their efforts to safeguard their computer systems against denial-of-service attacks from the Internet.

EPA Is a Major Steward of National Environmental Information

EPA's mission is to protect human health and safeguard the environment. The need to manage its programs for results substantially increases EPA's demand for high-quality environmental information. Such information is also required to identify and respond to emerging problems before significant damage is done to the environment. To fulfill its mission, EPA and the states collect a wealth of environmental data under various statutory and regulatory requirements. In addition, EPA conducts research

---

[3] *Information Security: Serious Weaknesses Place Critical Federal Operations and Assets at Risk* (GAO/AIMD-98-92, September 23, 1998).

[4] *High-Risk Series: Information Management and Technology* (GAO/HR-97-9, February 1997) and *High-Risk Series: An Update* (GAO/HR-99-1, January 1999).

[5] *Critical Infrastructure Protection: Comprehensive Strategy Can Draw on Year 2000 Experiences* (GAO/AIMD-00-1, October 1, 1999).

[6] *Defending America's Cyberspace: National Plan for Information Systems Protection: An Invitation to a Dialogue,* issued by the President on January 7, 2000.

on environmental issues and collects data through its own environmental monitoring activities.

EPA's major program offices—the offices of Water; Air and Radiation; Research and Development; Solid Waste and Emergency Response; and Prevention, Pesticides and Toxic Substances—are responsible for implementing pertinent statutes, such as the Clean Air Act and the Clean Water Act. An assistant administrator heads each program office. Ten regional offices, headed by regional administrators, assist in executing the agency's programs and determine regional needs within selected states. Also, administrative offices, including the Office of the Chief Financial Officer and OEI, headed by assistant administrators or their equivalents, support the overall mission of the agency.

EPA has spent significant time and resources to develop its information systems and computer networks to assist in carrying out its mission—reportedly $435 million and $403 million in fiscal years 1998 and 1999, respectively, for data collection and information management and technology operations and investments. The integrity and availability of the information maintained on EPA computers is important since it is used to support EPA's analyses, research, and regulatory activities.

Because of the nature of its mission, EPA collects, oversees, and disseminates data of varying sensitivity. EPA makes much of its information available to the public through Internet access in order to encourage public awareness and participation in managing human health and environmental risks and to meet statutory requirements. EPA also maintains confidential data from private businesses, data of varying sensitivity on human health and environmental risks, financial and contract data, and personal information on its employees. Consequently, EPA's information security program must accommodate the often competing goals of making much of its environmental information widely accessible while maintaining data integrity, availability, and appropriate confidentiality.

Like many other organizations, EPA's computer environment has changed over the last few years from one involving a centralized mainframe with a highly controlled network to one involving many large computers on a network with nearly unlimited access, including public access through the Internet. This new environment is beneficial because it provides EPA opportunities for streamlining operations and it has provided public access to significant amounts of information. However, this increasingly interconnected computing environment also significantly elevates the risks of inappropriate access to sensitive and critical data. These risks include exposing EPA computers and data to individuals with malicious or criminal intentions, who may want to disrupt or misuse EPA's systems for purposes such as fraud, sabotage, or obtaining sensitive business or personnel data. As a result, EPA, like many other private and government organizations, faces the challenge of balancing the benefits of new technology and Internet use with the new risks such technology introduces. Because such risks cannot be completely eliminated, this balancing act requires a proactive approach to managing information security risks that is dynamic and constantly attentive to changing threats.

EPA's System Access Controls Were Ineffective

Computer systems access controls are key to ensuring that only authorized individuals can gain access to sensitive and critical agency data. They include a variety of tools such as passwords, which are intended to authenticate authorized users; access control software, which is used to specify individual users' privileges on the system (e.g., read, alter, copy, or delete files); and firewalls, which are to serve as barriers for filtering out unwanted access.

Our tests showed that EPA's access controls were ineffective in adequately reducing the risk of intrusions and misuse. Using widely available software tools, we demonstrated that EPA's network was highly susceptible to intrusions through the Internet and that user and system administrator passwords could be easily accessed, read, or guessed. In addition, we identified weaknesses in all of EPA's computer operating systems that made it possible for intruders, as well as EPA employees or contractors, to bypass or disable computer access controls and undertake a wide variety of inappropriate or malicious acts. These acts could include tampering with data; browsing sensitive information; using EPA's computer resources for inappropriate purposes, such as launching attacks on other organizations; and seriously disrupting or disabling computer-supported operations.

Because the weaknesses we identified were associated with the operating systems of EPA's main computers and agencywide network—resources that are referred to as "general support systems"—they affected the security of all of the EPA operations that rely on them. These operations include computer applications that EPA's individual units rely on to carry out their day-to-day operations, such as gathering data on pollutants, research, regulatory enforcement, and financial management.

In short, we identified weaknesses that if exploited, could have allowed us to control individual EPA computer applications and the data used by these applications. As such, we could have copied, changed, deleted, or destroyed information, thus rendering any security controls implemented for software applications used in specific EPA office networks virtually ineffective. The most significant problems identified by our work are discussed below.

Ineffective Perimeter Defenses

A firewall and similar perimeter defenses are an organization's first line of defense from outside intrusion. Put simply, a firewall is a software package that controls the content of inbound and outbound computer network traffic, allowing only authorized traffic through its filters. If a firewall is not properly deployed, it may be overly restrictive, thus unnecessarily hindering the flow of network traffic, or it may be too weak, thus providing little or no protection. EPA's firewall and other perimeter defenses (referred to as screening routers)—designed largely to protect agency systems from unauthorized access from the Internet—were not effective in preventing such intrusions because of weaknesses in their configuration and deployment. In our tests, we simulated the type of attacks that might be employed by a computer hacker intruding via the Internet and readily breached and took control of EPA's firewall and other perimeter defenses, thereby gaining access to EPA's agencywide network.

Weak Network and Operating System Controls

In addition to having ineffective perimeter defenses, EPA did not have adequate controls over access to key network components. During our tests, we were able to move throughout the network unimpeded and could have diverted, altered, or disrupted network traffic. Further, we gained access to EPA's major computer systems and the applications supported by them. As a result, by intruding from the Internet, we could have browsed, altered, or deleted data associated with these applications or disrupted their operation.

Poor Password Protections

Passwords are EPA's primary means of ensuring that access to key network components is appropriately restricted to authorized personnel. However, we identified serious weaknesses in EPA's controls over the confidentiality and integrity of its passwords. For example, we were able to guess many of EPA's passwords based on our knowledge of commonly used passwords, and we were able to decrypt encrypted password files by using commonly available "password-cracking" software. While on the network, we eavesdropped on computer users' activities, observed them keying in passwords, and used these passwords to obtain "high level" system administration privileges. Such privileges would have allowed us to (1) change system access and other rules, (2) potentially read, alter, delete, or redirect network traffic, and (3) read or tamper with files maintained on EPA's larger computers.

Recent Remediation Efforts

Our audit has provided EPA's senior management with specific information on individual control weaknesses, and EPA has moved promptly to address these weaknesses. In a meeting with senior OEI management and technical staff in December 1999, we alerted EPA to significant security vulnerabilities identified by our testing, which, because of their severity, warranted immediate remediation by EPA. This interaction was productive and resulted in quick corrective actions.

Further, in mid-February, EPA began a series of more comprehensive efforts to supplement its information security controls and ensure the effectiveness of those in place. In addition, as an interim step to reduce its risks, EPA temporarily disabled its link to the Internet and discontinued certain services and access privileges while it (1) assessed the relative criticality and sensitivity of its computer-supported operations, (2) reevaluated the agency's and its customers' needs for access to data, and (3) implemented strengthened controls. While we have not retested EPA controls and, therefore, cannot attest to the effectiveness of its recent improvement efforts, EPA's actions demonstrate that it is moving in the right direction and taking a systematic, risk-based approach. Such an approach is important in helping to ensure that improvement efforts are effective and appropriate. As discussed later in this report, it is important that these efforts to strengthen technical controls be supported by improvements in the way EPA manages information security on an ongoing basis.

EPA's Systems and Data Have Been Compromised and Misused

EPA's records show that vulnerabilities, such as those just described, have been exploited by both external and internal sources. In some cases, these vulnerabilities were exploited because EPA had not corrected known vulnerabilities and properly managed user accounts. Further, those records illustrate deficiencies in EPA's ability to detect, respond to, and document security incidents affecting its systems.

The records we analyzed consist primarily of security-related problem reports for 1998 and 1999 that EPA extracted for us from a computerized database maintained at its National Computer Center. By analyzing the database and related records, we identified about two dozen instances where security weaknesses were exploited and EPA systems were compromised or misused. EPA's records, while incomplete for many incidents, show that some incidents resulted in damage, disruption, and criminal investigations. In addition, the records showed that EPA was the subject of repeated systematic probes from a variety of domestic and foreign sources. Both the nature and routine pattern of these probes are characteristic of attempts to identify vulnerabilities in EPA's computer network. Such activity raises concerns that intruders may be preparing for future penetrations.

Some examples that illustrate the types of intrusions and misuse we identified follow. These examples were taken from EPA's records; we did not independently investigate them. For many of the examples, we could not determine the full extent of any damage caused by the incidents or how the incidents were resolved because this information had not been documented in EPA's records. For other examples, details cannot be publicly disclosed because the incidents are currently under investigation.

- In June 1998, EPA was notified that one of its computers was used by a remote intruder as a means of gaining unauthorized access to a state university's computers. The problem report stated that vendor-supplied software updates were available to correct the vulnerability, but EPA had not installed them.
- In July 1999, a "chat room" was set up on a network server at one of EPA's regional financial management centers for hackers to post notes and, in effect, conduct on-line electronic conversations. According to EPA, this incident was still under investigation in mid-January of this year.
- In February 1999, a sophisticated penetration affected three of EPA's computers. EPA was unaware of this penetration until notified by the Federal Bureau of Investigation.
- In June 1999, an intruder penetrated an Internet web server at EPA's National Computer Center by exploiting a control weakness specifically identified by EPA about 3 years earlier during a previous penetration on a different system. The vulnerability continued to exist because EPA had not implemented vendor software updates (patches), some of which had been available since 1996.

- On two occasions during 1998, extraordinarily large volumes of network traffic—synonymous with a commonly used denial-of-service hacker technique—affected computers at one of EPA's field offices. In one case, an Internet user significantly slowed EPA's network activity and interrupted network service for over 450 EPA computer users. In a second case, an intruder used EPA computers to successfully launch a denial-of-service attack against an Internet service provider.
- In September 1999, an individual gained access to an EPA computer and altered the computer's access controls, thereby blocking authorized EPA employees from accessing files. This individual was no longer officially affiliated with EPA at the time of the intrusion, indicating a serious weakness in EPA's process for applying changes in personnel status to computer accounts.

Poor Intrusion Detection and Incident Response Capabilities Further Impair EPA's Security

Even strong controls may not block all intrusions and misuse, but organizations can reduce the risks associated with such events if they promptly take steps to detect intrusions and misuse before significant damage can be done. In addition, accounting for and analyzing security problems and incidents are effective ways for organizations to gain a better understanding of threats to their information and of the costs of their security-related problems. Such analyses can pinpoint vulnerabilities that need to be addressed to help ensure that they will not be exploited again. In this regard, problem and incident reports can provide valuable input for risk assessments, help in prioritizing security improvement efforts, and be used to illustrate risks and related trends in reports to senior management.

During our reviews of technical controls and of EPA's security problem and incident records, we identified a number of deficiencies in EPA's incident detection and handling capabilities.

- EPA's capabilities for detecting intrusions and misuse were very limited. The automated detection tools EPA had implemented were not effectively deployed, and in some instances, logs of computer activities were not promptly analyzed to identify unusual or suspicious events or patterns. The effect of these limitations was illustrated by the fact that EPA did not recognize and record much of the activity associated with our test activities. While 23 problem reports were recorded, indicating knowledge about our intrusion testing, none of them recognized the magnitude of our activity or the severity of the security breaches we initiated.

- For most of the instances where security weaknesses were actually exploited, EPA had not fully documented the extent of resulting damage or disclosure. Such information is helpful in better understanding security risks and in determining how much to spend on related controls.
- EPA did not routinely analyze problem reports to identify trends and vulnerabilities and apply lessons learned to other units throughout the agency.
- EPA did not fully follow up on problems to ensure that they were resolved and that identified vulnerabilities were not repeatedly exploited.
- Problem listings were not protected from browsing. Such protection is important to ensure that intruders or others cannot gain detailed information on security vulnerabilities awaiting correction or monitor the investigations of incidents that they may have originated.
- EPA had not established adequate standards, controls, responsibilities, and procedures to ensure uniform and complete management of security problems and responses or clearly differentiated government and contractor responsibilities.
- EPA had not routinely summarized and reported security problems and their resolutions to senior EPA managers so that they were aware of the magnitude of the problems and related trends.

EPA's incident recordkeeping procedures provide a beginning for more robust incident handling and analysis practices. However, the weaknesses described above diminish the value of these records and of related follow-up activities.

Security Program Planning and Management Are Fundamentally Weak

It is imperative that EPA correct the specific weaknesses we identified. However, ensuring that computer security controls remain effective on an ongoing basis will require substantial changes to the way EPA approaches information security, especially in regard to (1) assessing risk and determining security needs and (2) ensuring that existing controls are operating effectively. Our review of EPA's security planning and management process found that OEI, which includes EPA's Chief Information Officer, and EPA's program and support offices were not adequately working together to ensure that information security risks were fully understood and addressed.

The need for federal agencies to protect sensitive and critical, but unclassified, data has been recognized for years in various laws, including the Privacy Act of 1974, the Paperwork Reduction Act of 1980, and the Computer Security Act of 1987. In particular, the Computer Security Act of 1987 requires federal agencies to establish security plans for all federal computer systems that contain sensitive information. Also, the Office of Management and Budget (OMB) Circular A-130, Appendix III, *Security of Federal Automated Information Resources,* notes that all agency systems merit some level of protection and requires agencies to implement controls commensurate with risk. It also requires agencies to ensure that these controls are reviewed at least every 3 years and directs senior program managers to formally authorize use of each system prior to its implementation and periodically thereafter.

Our own study of leading security management practices used in commercial and nonfederal settings serves to help pinpoint the significant weaknesses in EPA's computer security program management.[7] We found that these leading organizations manage their information security risks through a cycle of risk management activities. The basic framework—built on 16 specific practices—provides for risk management through an ongoing cycle of activities coordinated by a central focal point. This management process, shown in figure 1, involves

- assessing risk to determine information security needs,
- developing and implementing policies and controls that meet these needs,
- promoting awareness to ensure that risks and responsibilities are understood, and
- instituting an ongoing program of tests and evaluations to ensure that policies and controls are appropriate and effective.

---

[7] *Information Security Management: Learning From Leading Organizations* (GAO/AIMD-98-68, May 1998).

Figure 1: The Risk Management Cycle

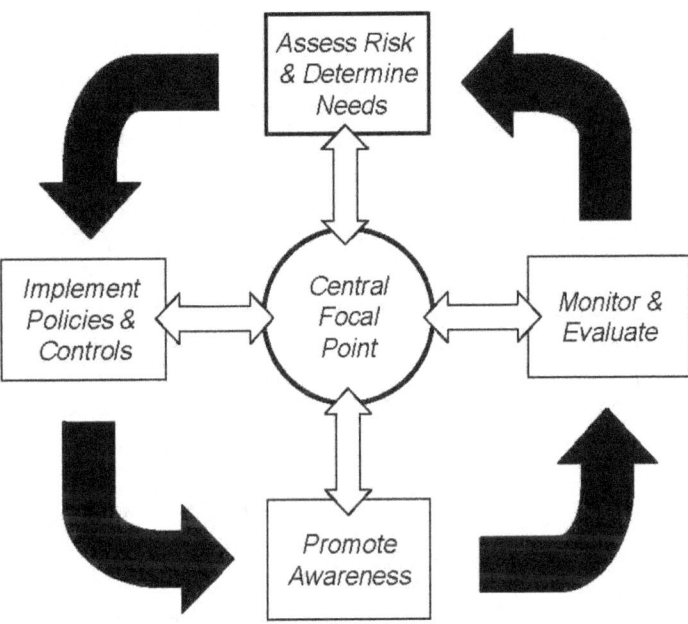

This process is generally consistent with OMB and National Institute of Standards and Technology (NIST) guidance on information security program management, and it has been endorsed by the federal Chief Information Officers Council as a useful resource for agency managers. By adopting the risk management principles and practices recommended by our guide, agencies can better protect their systems, detect attacks, and react to security breaches.

Risks Not Fully Considered

Conversely, EPA's security planning and management practices have been largely a paperwork exercise that has done little to substantively identify, evaluate, and mitigate risks. EPA's policies require each of its major program and support offices to

- determine what levels of protection are appropriate for data and systems supporting their mission-related operations;
- ensure that appropriate controls have been effectively implemented before systems become operational;

- describe information security program roles, responsibilities, and procedures consistent with the office's mission, including assigning responsibility to knowledgeable staff; and
- ensure that staff are provided security awareness training.

According to EPA policy, each unit's strategy for meeting these requirements is to be documented in information security program plans. Placing such responsibilities with EPA's individual program and support offices is appropriate because individual units are the most familiar with the sensitivity and criticality of their data and have the most to lose if poor security negatively affects their operations. Our review of individual office security plans and discussions with responsible officials found that many of EPA's major offices did not fully consider information security risks, clearly define the level of protection needed for their operations, or ensure that controls were implemented effectively. In particular, most offices did not adequately consider the security risks associated with the operating systems and agencywide network upon which their individual applications and information systems heavily rely. Nor did they consider other factors affecting the security of their individual systems, such as interfaces with other users' systems. For example, information security plans for some financial applications did not address the risks associated with other financial systems or other program offices' applications that transmit sensitive financial information.

In addition, EPA offices did not consistently apply the data risk categories, or sensitivity levels, described in EPA policy as the basis for determining what information security controls were needed. Some offices applied other categories or only partially applied EPA's guidance. For example, at the six offices for which security plans had been finalized, none identified the overall system sensitivity rating required to determine which set of minimum control requirements outlined in EPA agencywide guidance was appropriate for the systems.

Further, senior officials authorized some systems for processing without testing access controls to ensure that they had been implemented and were operating effectively. Twenty-eight of the 54 system security plans we reviewed had received no management authorization. Such authorizations are important because, according to OMB and EPA guidance, they are intended to represent management's determination that the security of the systems supporting their operations is adequate.

Central Security Management Functions Are Inadequate

While EPA program and mission-support offices bear much of the responsibility for ensuring that systems supporting their operations are adequately and effectively protected, EPA's OEI, which encompasses agency-level information technology management and information security activities, has an essential role in providing the needed technical expertise and in effectively implementing technical controls.[8] Our studies of security practices at leading organizations have shown that information security is a responsibility that must be shared by both technical and program staff. This is because, while program offices are in the best position to identify their most sensitive and critical operations and assets, they usually need assistance from technical personnel and security specialists who have current knowledge of the latest threats and of the range of technical controls that can be applied. As in many organizations, most of EPA's technical staff and security specialists who support the agencywide network are organizationally placed under the Assistant Administrator of OEI, who also serves as EPA's Chief Information Officer.

We found that OEI and its predecessor organization, which was under the Office of Administration and Resources Management, had not proactively monitored the effectiveness of information security efforts throughout the agency or provided adequate assistance to program offices. While an office within OEI had developed agencywide security policies and conducted some security-related training, neither that office nor any other EPA office has undertaken the role of facilitating and coordinating implementation of EPA's security policies throughout the agency or ensuring that all systems are periodically tested to ensure that controls are operating effectively.

Our study of leading organizations found that a strong central focal point was important to ensuring that policies were consistently understood and implemented and that risks, including those associated with agencywide networks and other broadly used support systems, were fully understood and considered in individual office plans. In its current formulation, OEI's structural organization and staffing capacity simply do not adequately

---

[8]The Paperwork Reduction Act of 1995 and the Clinger-Cohen Act of 1996 stipulate that agency heads are directly responsible for information technology management, including ensuring that the information security policies, procedures, and practices of their agencies are adequate. These acts also require the appointment of chief information officers for all federal agencies to help provide the expertise needed to implement effective information resources management.

address the requisite elements of an effective agencywide security program.

While the agencywide information security policy and guidance developed by OEI generally complied with OMB guidance, we identified several areas where it could be supplemented and clarified to help ensure more effective security program management at both the individual office level and EPA-wide. Specifically, EPA's information security policy, procedures, and guidance did not

- clearly distinguish between mandatory and optional requirements;
- define practical risk assessment procedures;
- clearly define responsibilities of Senior Information Resource Management Officers, system managers, information managers, or application owners, or describe staff's responsibility and involvement in plan development;
- establish an entitywide or office self-assessment process; or
- establish an entitywide process for monitoring resolution of identified security vulnerabilities.

These deficiencies are in addition to those previously described related to EPA incident handling capabilities.

EPA Has an Opportunity to Build on Its Ongoing Information Security Initiatives

The problems we identified pose significant challenges for EPA's entire executive and senior management ranks. The agency established OEI in October 1999 to improve the way it generally manages the large amounts of information it collects and maintains. While this reorganization may result in benefits in other areas of information management, at the close of our review, it had not yet significantly changed the way information security was being managed and addressed throughout the agency.

Planned improvements to the way EPA manages information security were outlined in a January 28, 2000, memorandum to EPA executives from the Principal Deputy Assistant Administrator for OEI. These included (1) an effort by the Office of Information Collection within OEI to take a broader look at the agency's information protection policies, particularly how the sensitivity of information is determined, and (2) establishment of a "Technical Information Security Staff" to rapidly enhance EPA's technical approach to information security. The memorandum identified the new security staff's key functions as

- developing technical approaches and implementation policies,
- researching and synthesizing best practices,
- supporting senior managers in understanding and carrying out their information security roles,
- educating users and technical staff,
- developing processes and procedures for tracking and reporting security incidents, and
- overseeing the auditing and effectiveness of security programs.

These provisions address many of the management deficiencies we identified, and we encourage EPA to move forward in implementing them. However, effective implementation will require joint efforts by both program and technical staff and a major adjustment in the way EPA considers information security risks and in its management approach. The Technical Information Security Staff will face major challenges in facilitating communication and cooperation among EPA's (1) National Computer Center staff, (2) program, financial, and regional officials, and (3) the various components of OEI. It will be essential that the new security staff proactively oversee and coordinate security-related activities throughout EPA and ensure that controls are periodically tested, especially those controls that protect the most sensitive and critical of EPA's data.

Conclusion

EPA is confronted with significant computer security problems that threaten its operations and data. Many of these problems pertain to specific technical control issues and EPA's security incident handling capabilities. These weaknesses require immediate attention, and EPA has begun steps to address them. However, like other organizations—public and private—ensuring that these improvements continue to be effective and implementing a sustainable information security program will require top management support and leadership, disciplined processes, consistent oversight, and, perhaps, additional levels of technical and funding support. EPA has also begun efforts to implement these important management practices. It is important that these efforts be institutionalized and sustained in the long term.

Recommendations

Control Weaknesses

We recommend that the EPA Administrator direct EPA's Principal Deputy Assistant Administrator for the Office of Environmental Information to complete efforts to develop and implement an action plan for strengthening access controls associated with EPA's major computer operating systems and agencywide network. This will require ongoing cooperative efforts between EPA's Office of Environmental Information and EPA's program and regional offices. We provided EPA a detailed list of these control weaknesses and related recommendations in the Limited Official Use report.

Incident Handling

We recommend that the Administrator direct EPA's Principal Deputy Assistant Administrator for the Office of Environmental Information, the assistant administrators, and the regional administrators to

- implement policy and procedures for monitoring suspicious activity in log files and audit trails on a regular schedule commensurate with current threats and potential impact of damage or disruption and
- restrict access to security incident data so that only those individuals involved in monitoring and investigating incidents can view such data.

To strengthen EPA's ongoing security posture and incident management efforts, we recommend that the Administrator direct EPA's Principal Deputy Assistant Administrator for the Office of Environmental Information to

- develop, document, and enforce standards, controls, and procedures for security intrusion and misuse detection, recording, response, follow-up, analysis, and reporting, including clear assignment of responsibilities for government and contractor employees to ensure appropriate oversight of security functions;
- analyze existing and future problem reports to identify deficiencies in system controls, incident records, and problem responses; and
- periodically report summaries of security incidents and responses to senior EPA and application managers in order to raise awareness of security risks, ensure that response actions and control improvements are appropriately managed, and ensure that the related risks are considered in security planning.

Security Program Planning and Management

We recommend that the Administrator direct EPA's Principal Deputy Assistant Administrator for the Office of Environmental Information, the assistant administrators for other EPA offices, and the regional administrators to work together to

- identify and rank their information assets and computer-supported operations according to their sensitivity and criticality to EPA's mission;
- determine what level of protection is appropriate to adequately reduce the information security risks associated with these operations and assets;
- select procedures and controls that provide this protection;
- identify and prioritize improvement actions needed; and
- implement a program of routine and periodic testing and evaluation of the procedures and controls adopted, with emphasis on those procedures and controls affecting the most sensitive and critical information assets.

We also recommend that the Administrator direct EPA's Principal Deputy Assistant Administrator for the Office of Environmental Information to

- proactively assist EPA offices in understanding and implementing EPA's agencywide information security policy;
- assist EPA program and regional offices in understanding the information security risks associated with their operations, including those risks stemming from their reliance on general support systems, such as the agencywide network maintained by EPA's National Computer Center;
- assist offices in developing and implementing plans for testing key information security controls associated with systems under their control;
- develop and implement plans for testing key information security controls associated with general support systems and other systems under their control;
- monitor progress in implementing actions needed to address identified information security weaknesses;
- periodically report to the Administrator and the heads of EPA program and support offices on the effectiveness of EPA's information security program; and
- adjust and supplement EPA's written information security policies and related guidance to include information that
  - clarifies which elements of policies and related guidance are mandatory and which are optional,

- defines information security roles and responsibilities, and
- defines procedures and provides tools for agencywide self-assessments.

Agency Comments and Our Evaluation

In written comments on a draft of this report, EPA's Principal Deputy Assistant Administrator for the Office of Environmental Information concurred with our recommendations and described EPA's corrective actions. According to the comments, EPA has taken steps to strengthen access controls, enhance its intrusion detection capabilities, and improve its information security management structure. Further, EPA's plans include

- establishing a program for testing and evaluating the controls and procedures adopted,
- improving the risk assessment process, and
- better supporting program managers in carrying out their information security related responsibilities.

We cannot yet draw conclusions on the effectiveness of EPA's actions because many have not yet been fully implemented and others have not been independently tested. However, the corrective actions described represent a comprehensive approach to improving EPA's agencywide information security program and, if implemented effectively, should significantly strengthen EPA's security posture. To be effective on an ongoing basis, it is important that EPA's efforts be institutionalized as part of a continual cycle of risk management activity. In this regard, the periodic tests and evaluations that EPA plans to implement should provide EPA management with important information on the success of its actions and provide a basis for fine-tuning the agency's security program in the future.

As agreed with your office, unless you publicly announce the contents of this report earlier, we plan no further distribution until 30 days from the date of this letter. At that time, we will send copies to Senator Max Baucus, Senator Christopher S. Bond, Senator Robert C. Byrd, Senator Pete V. Domenici, Senator Richard J. Durbin, Senator Frank Lautenberg, Senator Joseph Lieberman, Senator Barbara A. Mikulski, Senator Bob Smith, Senator Ted Stevens, Senator Fred Thompson, and Senator George V. Voinovich, and to Representative Dan Burton, Representative John D. Dingell, Representative Stephen Horn, Representative John R. Kasich, Representative Alan B. Mollohan, Representative David R. Obey,

Representative John Spratt, Representative Jim Turner, Representative James T. Walsh, Representative Henry A. Waxman, and Representative C.W. Bill Young in their capacities as Chairmen or Ranking Minority Members of Senate and House Committees and Subcommittees. We are also sending copies to the Honorable Carol M. Browner, Administrator, Environmental Protection Agency; the Honorable Nikki L. Tinsley, Inspector General, Environmental Protection Agency; the Honorable Jacob J. Lew, Director, Office of Management and Budget; and other agency officials. Copies will be made available to others upon request.

If you have questions regarding this report, please contact me at (202) 512-6240 or by e-mail at mcclured.aimd@gao.gov.

Sincerely yours,

David L. McClure
Associate Director
Defense and Governmentwide
 Information Systems

Objectives, Scope, and Methodology

Our objectives were to (1) test the effectiveness of key computer-based controls over access to and use of EPA's systems, (2) determine the extent and impact of reported computer security incidents involving EPA's systems and related EPA responses, and (3) evaluate EPA's agencywide computer security program planning and management. To accomplish these objectives, we applied appropriate sections of our *Federal Information System Controls Audit Manual* (GAO/AIMD-12.19.6), which describes our methodology for reviewing information system controls that affect the integrity, confidentiality, and availability of computerized data associated with federal agency operations.

To test the effectiveness of key controls over EPA computer systems, we examined the configuration and control implementation for each of the computer operating systems and for the agencywide computer network that support most of EPA's mission-related and financial operations. In addition, we attempted to penetrate EPA's systems through the Internet from a remote location, and we attempted to exploit identified control weaknesses to verify the vulnerability they presented. We also met with officials at EPA's National Computer Center to discuss their practices in managing the security of EPA's systems, possible reasons for vulnerabilities identified, and plans for future improvement.

To determine the extent and impact of security incidents involving EPA systems, we reviewed reports of computer security incidents from 1992 through 1999 identified by EPA's IG and analyzed listings of security problem reports for 1998 and 1999 provided by EPA's National Computer Center. Based on this analysis, we identified and characterized notable individual incidents, patterns and trends for recent incidents, and ambiguities and omissions in reported incident data and incident management actions. To evaluate EPA's practices for responding to incidents, we (1) reviewed EPA's policy and procedures on incident management, (2) examined security problem reports to determine whether they accurately reflected the testing activities we performed, and (3) discussed incident management practices with EPA's National Computer Center, OEI, and IG officials.

To evaluate EPA's agencywide information security program planning and management, we reviewed pertinent agencywide policies, guidance, and security plans and held discussions with officials responsible for developing and implementing these policies and plans throughout EPA. This included

- analyzing agencywide policies to determine (1) their compliance with OMB and NIST guidance and (2) whether they incorporated the management best practices identified in our executive guide *Information Security Management: Learning From Leading Organizations* (GAO/AIMD-98-68, May 1998);
- meeting with officials in EPA's OEI, which is responsible for managing EPA's information security program, to determine what actions it has taken to ensure effective security program implementation;
- discussing security plan development and implementation with officials in EPA's Office of the Chief Financial Officer and five of the agency's program area offices: the Office of Air and Radiation; the Office of Prevention, Pesticides and Toxic Substances; the Office of Research and Development; the Office of Solid Waste and Emergency Response; and the Office of Water; and
- reviewing 54 finalized system security plans from four program offices, OEI, and the Office of the Chief Financial Officer to determine if they conformed with EPA's agencywide policies and complied with OMB and NIST guidance.

We performed our audit work at EPA headquarters and at EPA's National Computer Center from September 1999 through February 2000 in accordance with generally accepted government auditing standards. EPA's Principal Deputy Assistant Administrator for OEI provided comments on a draft of this report. These comments are discussed in the "Agency Comments and Our Evaluation" section of this report and are reprinted in appendix II.

Comments From the Environmental Protection Agency

UNITED STATES ENVIRONMENTAL PROTECTION AGENCY
WASHINGTON, D.C. 20460

JUN 15 2000

OFFICE OF
ENVIRONMENTAL INFORMATION

Mr. Jeffrey C. Steinhoff
Assistant Comptroller General
Accounting and Information Management Division
United States General Accounting Office
Washington, D.C. 20548

Dear Mr. Steinhoff:

Thank you for the opportunity to review the draft report entitled, "Information Security: Fundamental Weaknesses Place EPA Data and Operations at Risk," GAO-AIMD-00-215. We appreciate the General Accounting Office's (GAO's) comprehensive assessment of EPA's information security systems and the professionalism that was shown to EPA by GAO staff auditors throughout this process.

As you know, EPA has had an information security program in place for several years and has been continuously working to enhance our ability to address security concerns. We were aware of several technical problems requiring both short-term and long-term corrective action and had already begun addressing these issues prior to February, when we temporarily shut down our Internet web site to accelerate these enhancements.

We had installed a formal firewall for public access and had planned for a final formal firewall and other intrusion detection enhancements to be completed by Spring 2000. Upon learning about potential vulnerabilities in our systems, we expedited our plans and immediately began to implement a number of aggressive, corrective responses during these past few months. We believe we have demonstrated a strong commitment to protect the confidentiality, integrity, and availability of our information while at the same time, maintaining EPA's ability to conduct the business of the Agency -- that of protecting human health and the environment.

Your report which summarizes your Agencies detailed security test and evaluation of our wide area network (WAN), associated resources, and information security management and organizational practices challenges EPA to make a number of improvements in our information security program. We take these challenges seriously and have made concerted efforts to implement improvements as quickly as possible, and appreciate your recognition of our efforts.

Internet Address (URL) • http://www.epa.gov
Recycled/Recyclable • Printed with Vegetable Oil Based Inks on Recycled Paper (Minimum 30% Postconsumer)

Even though we have made many enhancements in our program since the first of the year, we recognize that the Agency must continue to improve our security procedures, to hold the Agency's senior managers accountable for overseeing these procedures, and to upgrade our technology. We have already begun to enhance our policies, technology, and practices to protect the information on which the Agency and the public depends, and are pledged to sustain this effort. Enclosed are our comments on the draft report and a summary of our progress to date.

Once again, thank you for providing us with critical information to enable EPA to make improvements in our information security program and systems. EPA wants to continue to work with GAO and welcomes any additional suggestions and guidance that will help us to achieve the Agency's information security goals.

Please feel free to contact me at (202) 564-6665, or Mark Day, Deputy CIO and Director, Office of Technology Operations and Planning, at (202) 260-4465, if you or your staff have any questions or require additional clarification or information.

Sincerely,

Margaret N. Schneider
Principal Deputy Assistant Administrator

Attachment

Comments - Draft GAO Report   Page 1

Background:

As noted in GAO's report, over recent years, EPA's computer environment has evolved from an environment that was largely mainframe oriented with a controlled network with little or no connection to the world beyond EPA's State partners. However, with the explosive growth of the Internet and the transition to a computer network, EPA became connected to the entire world. This fundamentally changed EPA's risks and security needs in ways not immediately obvious.

As many recent events have shown, all organizations including EPA, must reevaluate the inherent security issues that derive from open access to the Internet. This creates many changes for the way government agencies, business, and other organizations conduct their operations. To address these concerns, EPA has found that while we must continue to make information available to fulfill our duties, it must be done using a new security paradigm which recognizes that integrity and denial of service threats are greatly heightened with the use of the Internet. This new paradigm is essentially closing EPA's entire network and then allowing only very specific uses to be opened with appropriate controls. This is a major cultural change for all public information oriented Agencies, not just EPA, which will take some time to be fully incorporated into the culture.

Prior to the time of the most recent GAO audit and subsequent brief shut down of EPA's Internet site, EPA had committed to making a variety of changes in security systems and had begun to plan for and implement several of them. EPA also made many security improvements over the past decade in response to previous Office of Inspector General audits, including:

- implemented Resource Access Control Facility (RACF) mainframe controls when the mainframe was our main platform;
- adopted many, but not all of the Computer Emergency Response Team (CERT) advisories as we moved into use of the Internet;
- installed a router based firewall, at a time when that was appropriate;
- installed private separate networks for confidential systems holding critical trade secret information;
- developed an information security planning policy and program;
- installed a formal firewall for public access; and
- planned for a final formal firewall and intrusion detection capabilities.

Despite the measures EPA had taken and planned, EPA realized, based on the current technological environment and GAO's findings, that there is more to do.

Responses to Specific Audit Recommendations:

For the past several months, EPA has been implementing both immediate, short-term solutions to control emergency system access issues, and at the same time, planning for and beginning to address more permanent security solutions and controls to address threats to our information.

Comments - Draft GAO Report Page 2

Immediately following our decision to briefly disconnect EPA's internal network from the Internet, we began implementing numerous security improvements including: installing an additional firewall; making greater use of intrusion detection and encryption tools; and certifying compliance of controls and password protections, just to name a few. While continuing to systematically restore services, we have had to balance these immediate service needs with our additional responsibilities to analyze and develop a more formal plan for protecting the Agency's information resources.

To do both short-term emergency response and long-term planning at the same time has been demanding on both EPA's employee and contractor staff. Despite these multiple assignments, the Office of Environmental Information (OEI) has been developing a detailed, comprehensive plan to improve the Agency's information security controls and the overall information security program, and expects to complete the plan's first version by June 30, 2000. Given the complexity of the issues, the preliminary time estimates for the various efforts are described in the following way:

- Near-term - within 6 months
- Mid-term - within 6 months to one year
- Long-term - beyond one year

Following are EPA's responses to specific recommendations outlined in the draft report. Measures already taken, those we plan to take, and the general time frame by which we plan to complete the effort are identified.

<u>Control Weaknesses</u>

GAO Control Weakness Recommendation - *EPA's Administrator direct the Acting Assistant Administrator for the Office of Environmental Information to complete efforts to develop and implement an action plan for strengthening access controls associated with EPA's major computer operating systems and Agency wide network. This will require ongoing cooperative efforts between EPA's Office of Environmental Information and EPA's Program and Regional offices.*

EPA Action:
EPA has taken a number of immediate steps to strengthen access controls. To address GAO's preliminary findings on February 17, 2000, the Administrator made a decision to physically disconnect EPA's internal network from the Internet until full firewall protections were in place. This decision, while causing substantial disruption to Agency business operations, helped us to establish a baseline set of firewall business rules, providing significantly improved security from external threats, ahead of the originally planned time frame of April 2000. Once the full firewall was in place and using a risk-based approach, EPA:

Comments - Draft GAO Report   Page 3

- re-established specific, limited Internet uses in a very deliberate, tested, and controlled manner either on an interim basis with compensating controls, as necessary, or as a final, secure implementation;
- re-established a baseline of trusted host systems and network controls for reducing risks from known and potential earlier compromises;
- initiated a comprehensive, Agency-wide process for recertification of external access requirements for network and host applications;
- has been restoring services in an orderly fashion to ensure appropriate security controls were identified, operational, and maintained to reduce the risk potential for unauthorized network access, penetration, and/or information compromise; and
- is re-evaluating these interim solutions in light of GAO's findings and working on adopting and implementing more permanent solutions.

Concurrently, OEI directed an accelerated strengthening of the Agency firewall protecting the public access portion of the network. The firewall rules protecting the public access component of the network are now based on our assessment of the risks (including GAO findings) and our business needs commensurate with public access requirements.

In addition to formal firewalls, EPA severely restricted external border routers consistent with the basic CERT approach of denial of all traffic except what is permitted for business reasons. EPA is increasing the level of authentication required and has begun a network segmentation process. Where necessary, EPA has implemented compensating controls for issues representing potential security risks to implement more of a defense-in-depth security philosophy.

OEI provided leadership, technical support and guidance for Agency-wide efforts to improve various technical controls. Examples include recertification of system controls, user identification, improved authentication, least-privilege access control settings of critical assets, virus protection and password management.

Personnel security requirements and the governing background investigation policy for both Federal users and contractor users are currently under review. EPA has begun more thorough background security screening for federal users with privileged access such as system administrators and users who require access to certain types of sensitive information. EPA has begun the necessary work for more thorough contractor background screening as well.

The new OEI organization and the consolidation of the headquarters LAN management have enabled substantial strengthening of security measures for the central infrastructure. OEI is working with EPA's program and regional partners to extend this success to all EPA assets.

Incident Handling

GAO Incident Handling Recommendation 1 - *EPA's Administrator direct the Acting Assistant Administrator for the Office of Environmental Information, the Assistant Administrators, and the Regional Administrators to implement policy and procedures for monitoring suspicious activity*

Comments - Draft GAO Report Page 4

*in log files and audit trails on a regular schedule commensurate with current threats and
potential impact of damage or disruption.*

EPA Action:
To improve our ability to monitor for suspicious activity, on February 22, 2000, OEI requested
that all Agency organization heads confirm their organization had implemented basic EPA
information security policy and directives on password management, technical controls, and
management controls by March 24th. These controls included audit settings and review
procedures including daily audit log reviews. The responses have been reviewed and a corrective
action approach is underway where limited deficiencies were noted. EPA has written procedures
for its log reviews within its central environment. In the near-term, EPA will develop additional
procedures as needed for the remaining platforms and provide these to the programs and Regions.

GAO Incident Handling Recommendation 2 - *EPA's Administrator direct the Acting Assistant
Administrator for the Office of Environmental Information, the Assistant Administrators, and the
Regional Administrators to restrict access to security incident data so that only those individuals
involved in monitoring and investigating incidents can view such data.*

EPA Action:
The individual users who need access to security sensitive incident details and response
information has been analyzed and reduced by over 95%. In the mid-term, EPA will develop a
more formal process to manage access. In the long-term, OEI anticipates development of a
separate system to house security incident information.

GAO Incident Handling Recommendation 3 - *EPA's Administrator direct the Acting Assistant
Administrator for the Office of Environmental Information to develop, document and enforce
standards, controls, and procedures for security intrusion and misuse detection, recording,
response, follow-up, analysis, and reporting, including clear assignment of responsibilities for
Government and contractor employees to ensure appropriate oversight and security functions.*

EPA Action:
OEI has implemented additional hardware, software, and staff resources dedicated to enhancing
the Agency's intrusion detection (ID) capabilities. Intrusion detection systems have been
deployed to observe network activity both outside and inside the Agency firewalls. OEI has
committed the resources to provide for the daily review and analysis of logs for centrally managed
assets. The assignment of this responsibility has been made clear within OEI and its managed
contractors. A weekly summary report which includes ID activity is currently reviewed by OEI
senior management.

OEI has undertaken a risk-based assessment of the network to determine if profiles of
compromised computer systems are present in the Agency. The scanning, review and
establishment of a defined perimeter has been completed for both the Agency's North Carolina
central environment and the headquarters subnet containing the contractor CBI data system.
Work on our headquarters campus servers has begun and is scheduled for completion in the near-

Comments - Draft GAO Report   **Page 5**

term. In the near-term, EPA plans to complete a scan and review of all remaining headquarters and regional campus servers and establish appropriate campus perimeters to enhance our detection and containment capabilities. In the mid-term, EPA plans to scan and review all remaining assets and, in the long-term, periodically repeat scans and reviews of all assets. Beyond that, OEI will continue to provide more detailed risk assessments for specific programs at their request.

EPA has engaged outside, independent contractors to assess current ID capabilities, recommend incident handling procedures based on industry best practices, and suggest long-term strategies for improving ID and incident response procedures for completion in the near-term. Based on the results, an enhanced ID program will be developed which will clearly define the roles and responsibilities of government and contractor employees. Implementation of this program will begin in the near-term and be fully operational in the mid-term. Finally, EPA will formally document its standards, controls, and procedures in the long-term in Agency policy documents.

GAO Incident Handling Recommendation 4 - *EPA's Administrator direct the Acting Assistant Administrator for the Office of Environmental Information to analyze existing and future problem reports to identify deficiencies in system controls, incident records and problem responses.*

EPA Action:
EPA has begun this process. EPA already has a quick analysis of GAO's findings for multiple platforms to allow us to apply lessons learned across all platforms. We are also already working with our contractors and Inspector General's office to analyze problems and review logs to identify problems.

In the near-term, OEI will develop a process to receive regular incident reports from all programs and Regions, consolidate those reports and prepare summaries to be distributed to senior management. Also in the near-term, OEI will review the historical record of security incidents to identify trends.

In the mid-term, OEI will implement a formal program to periodically review and analyze problem reports that identify deficiencies in EPA system controls, incident records and problem responses. Throughout the process, OEI will distribute findings for identified deficiencies and corresponding compensating controls or Agency approved solutions to adequately address each deficiency.

GAO Incident Handling Recommendation 5 - *EPA's Administrator direct the Acting Assistant Administrator for the Office of Environmental Information to periodically report summaries of security incidents and responses to senior EPA and application managers in order to raise awareness of security risks, ensure that response actions and control improvements are appropriately managed, and ensure that the related risks are considered in security planning.*

Comments - Draft GAO Report   Page 6

EPA Action:
OEI is now reviewing and summarizing security incidents for senior management. The Deputy
CIO currently receives and reviews a weekly report on security incidents relating to EPA's
centrally managed resources. In the near-term OEI will also develop a tracking system to ensure
that response actions and control improvements are implemented. Security incident information
will be reviewed with appropriate members of the Agency's Quality and Information Council
(QIC), consisting of executive managers from EPA's program and regional offices, and with
appropriate application managers. In the mid-term, OEI will formally institute a process to
regularly evaluate incident reports to identify trends and relationships that will improve its ability
to anticipate new threats and vulnerabilities.

<u>Security Program Planning and Management</u>

GAO Security Program Planning and Management Recommendations 1 - 4 - *EPA's
Administrator direct the Acting Assistant Administrator for the Office of Environmental
Information and the Assistant Administrators for other EPA offices and the Regional
Administrators to work together to:*

- *identify and rank their information assets and computer-supported operations according
  to their sensitivity and criticality to the mission;*
- *determine what level of protection is appropriate to adequately reduce the information
  security risks associated with these operations and assets;*
- *select procedures and controls that provide protection; and*
- *identify and prioritize improvement actions needed.*

EPA Action:
EPA currently has information sensitivity criteria and controls. We will use and assess these
criteria and controls, evaluate risks, and make necessary changes and improvements as we learn
more.

EPA currently requires each office and Region to identify and rank their information assets as part
of the security planning process using established criteria for identification of information
sensitivity. EPA has established an Agency wide workgroup to further assess and amend, as
appropriate, the classification of the sensitivity of the Agency's information holdings and enhance
the policies and procedures for protecting the various classes. This work is expected to be
completed in the mid-term.

Based upon our current classes of information and immediately available controls, EPA has
selected procedures to provide the best protection possible. We based our priorities on the best
available information. For example, EPA has: 1) expanded its network segmentation over the
past three months by isolating traffic to the public access network from the Agency general
purpose network; 2) significantly reduced the potential for communications from the Internet to
the Agency's general purpose network; and 3) limited direct access from the Internet to internal

Comments - Draft GAO Report   Page 7

servers on the general purpose network to recertified and authenticated users via encrypted protocols.

In the near-term, the Agency will complete risk assessments of critical/priority systems and applications; apply current classification criteria and tools based on known risks; revisit the sensitivity classification criteria and required protection levels, focusing first on contract information; and develop a plan for conducting awareness/training sessions and enhancing implementation of information sensitivity criteria and guidelines.

In the mid-term, EPA will revise the classification scheme and protection tools as appropriate; harmonize these improvements; incorporate them into EPA policies, guidance and training; and provide implementation assistance.

In the long-term, EPA will evaluate the implementation of information sensitivity criteria and guidelines, and continually assess, on an annual basis, the need for new categories of data requiring protection, the efficacy of the existing tools, and whether additional tools are needed to address current and new threats.

GAO Security Program Planning and Management Recommendation 5, 8 and 9 - *EPA's Administrator direct the Acting Assistant Administrator for the Office of Environmental Information (and in recommendation 5, the first bullet - the Assistant Administrators for other EPA offices and the Regional Administrators to work together) to:*

- *implement a program of routine and periodic testing and evaluation of the procedures and controls adopted, with emphasis on those procedures and controls affecting the most sensitive and critical information assets.*
- *assist offices in developing and implementing plans for testing key information security controls associated with systems under their control; and*
- *develop and implement plans for testing key information security controls associated with general support systems and other systems under their control.*

EPA Action:
To test systems and controls, both for central and distributed assets and systems, EPA has already conducted a significant amount of testing. OEI has conducted scans of the headquarters and National Computer Center perimeters and conducted penetration testing of the firewall. EPA has also begun scans of Regional offices that will test the model for remote access. EPA will conduct follow-up testing of the Regions after remote access is implemented.

EPA has developed a three part approach to respond to these recommendations. First, our central operating division, under the Deputy CIO, will acquire and deploy, in the near-term, automated monitoring tools that will allow it to monitor compliance with configuration standards within OEI managed resources as well as in program offices and Regions. This will allow us to quickly identify any deviations from standards and take corrective actions. This will provide the first level of testing and control for all managers.

Comments - Draft GAO Report Page 8

Second, in the mid-term, EPA, through its Deputy CIO's Technical Information Security Staff, will implement a program of on-going penetration testing of its central resources and resources managed by programs and Regions. OEI will work with programs and Regions to identify the most sensitive information systems and general support systems. OEI will also assist the programs and Regions in interpreting the results of the tests and identifying any necessary corrective measures.

Finally, beginning in the long-term, the CIO's office will conduct a periodic (at least annual) review to evaluate the effectiveness of controls and identify weaknesses in the testing and monitoring procedures and program. This review will be an independent review of all other efforts.

GAO Security Program Planning and Management Recommendation 6 - *EPA's Administrator direct the Acting Assistant Administrator for the Office of Environmental Information to pro-actively assist EPA offices in understanding and implementing EPA's agency wide information security policy.*

EPA Action:
To assist senior managers in understanding EPA's policy, OEI:

- communicated basic security requirements to senior executives through memos from the Deputy Administrator and OEI Principal Deputy Assistant Administrator;
- conducted information security emergency awareness training for senior EPA career executives at QIC meetings;
- conducted an information security awareness training session for Agency senior political and career executives; and
- will pilot test, in the mid-term, a formal information security awareness training session for Agency managers; based on results of the pilot EPA will deliver additional information security awareness sessions for Agency managers.

To assist information security practitioners and Agency staff, OEI:

- established regular teleconferences with Agency primary Information Security Officers;
- will hold a training and awareness forum for all Agency Information Security Officers in the near-term;
- will provide a 2-week formal training for Agency central security staff and primary Information Security Officers in the near-term, and will continually assess the need to provide additional sessions;
- will provide information security awareness training for all Agency staff in the near-term;
- will provide training on implementation of specific technical controls in the near-term; will revise, in the mid-term, the awareness training materials for ISOs to use in their organizations on a continuing basis; and
- will incorporate information from the incident reporting program in awareness materials.

Comments - Draft GAO Report   Page 9

GAO Security Program Planning and Management Recommendation 7 - *EPA's*
Administrator direct the Acting Assistant Administrator for the Office of Environmental
Information to assist EPA program and Regional offices in understanding the information
security risks associated with their operations, including those risks stemming from their reliance
on general support systems, such as the agency wide network maintained by EPA's National
Computer Center.

EPA Action:
EPA is currently stepping-up efforts to improve the risk assessment process. OEI has begun the
process of conducting training, improving processes and procedures, and updating current
guidance for risk assessments. In the near-term, this risk assessment process will: 1) identify the
risks inherent in the central infrastructure; 2) provide training to those programs with systems
having the most sensitive trade secret and financial data; and 3) communicate those risks which
must be controlled in their systems and applications. In the mid-term, OEI will conduct training
for remaining Regions and programs. In the long-term, OEI will provide revised formal policy
and then begin periodic assessments of general support system risks as part of an ongoing
program to meet new risks and threats, update controls, and provide support to the programs in
their systems and applications planning. The assessment period will be based on modifications
and other risk factors, and will occur at least annually.

However, to fully improve the risk assessment process, more needs to be done on a Federal basis.
For example, there needs to be: 1) proactive feedback from law enforcement agencies in referred
cases; 2) greater sharing among agencies of shared risks from vendor products; 3) greater Federal
leadership in defining risks which are often shared and common; and 4) greater common
classifications of the levels of sensitivity of information among civilian agencies, analogous to
defense agencies' practices. EPA does not believe this is an issue that can be solved unilaterally.
OEI will continuously work with other agencies to improve the process.

GAO Security Program Planning and Management Recommendation 10 - *EPA's*
Administrator direct the Acting Assistant Administrator for the Office of Environmental
Information to monitor progress in implementing actions needed to address identified
information security weaknesses.

EPA Action:
OEI is already actively monitoring progress in implementing actions needed to address the
identified information security weaknesses, as outlined in the response to recommendations 5, 8,
and 9. As mentioned initially, EPA has begun development of a comprehensive plan with
prioritized milestones for additional security protection activities. In the near-term, EPA will have
an active tracking system with monthly reporting to the CIO and Assistant Administrator of OEI.

GAO Security Program Planning and Management Recommendation 11 - *EPA's*
Administrator direct the Acting Assistant Administrator for the Office of Environmental
Information to periodically report to the Administrator and the heads of EPA program and
support offices on the effectiveness of EPA's information security program.

Comments - Draft GAO Report   Page 10

EPA Action:
As described in the response to Recommendations 5, 8 and 9, in the long-term, the Assistant
Administrator will conduct an annual independent review to evaluate the effectiveness of controls
and identify weaknesses in the testing and monitoring procedures and program. These results will
be reported to the Administrator, the Assistant and Regional Administrators, and the Agency's
Quality and Information Council, using the Federal Managers' Financial Integrity Act (FMFIA)
process to focus attention on the most important areas of concern.

GAO Security Program Planning and Management Recommendation 12 - *EPA's
Administrator direct the Acting Assistant Administrator for the Office of Environmental
Information to adjust and supplement EPA's written information security policies and related
guidance to include clarifying which elements of policies and related guidance are mandatory
and which are optional; defining information security roles and responsibilities; and providing
tools for Agency wide risk assessments.*

EPA Action:
In May 2000, OEI issued a memo from the Director of the Office of Technology Operations and
Planning to Agency Information Security Officers detailing existing information on information
security roles and responsibilities. At that time, OEI also created an advisory group consisting of
information security staff and Agency Information Security Officers to further refine information
security roles and responsibilities.

OEI is undertaking a broad review of Agency policies and regulations related to information and
information security. Part of the process will entail revising policies so that they are easier to
understand and implement. OEI's goal is to ensure that these policies have clearly defined roles
and responsibilities, and that they make distinctions between mandatory policies and requirements,
and those which are recommended procedures and guidance. In the near-term, OEI will:

*   identify all policies needing to be revised and/or updated;
*   set priorities for updating and/or revising policies;
*   issue a final National Network Telecommunications Policy; and
*   issue a final policy on implementation of CERT advisories.

In the mid-term, OEI will target the highest priority policies for EPA's Agency wide clearance
process.

In the long-term, EPA will continue to revise its information security policies as necessary.

Additional Actions by EPA

The Agency has taken and plans to take other steps which, although they do not directly respond
to specific recommendations in the GAO draft report, will strengthen the security program.

Comments - Draft GAO Report   Page 11

First, as noted in the report, OEI created a new, high-level, Technical Information Security Staff (TISS), charged with central oversight over all aspects of Agency information security. The TISS has primary responsibilities for:

- developing technical approaches and implementation polices for information security;
- researching and analyzing government and industry security "best-practices;"
- supporting senior EPA managers in understanding and accomplishing their information security responsibilities;
- developing information security education and awareness training for Agency users and technical personnel;
- developing processes and procedures for tracking and reporting information security incidents and/or compromises; and
- overseeing the internal auditing and effectiveness of Agency information security programs, policies, and procedures.

Second, EPA has reprogrammed some of its very scarce resources to accelerate an enhancement of the security program. EPA is also continuing to pursue additional resources both for this year and future years.

Third, we have radically changed our overall approach to security, including Deputy CIO issuance of new directives to central staff on CERT advisory implementation, and a risk based process of formal review of access controls and firewall service rules before any service is restored from our shutdown of external connectivity.

Finally, one of the most important steps EPA can take to provide greater security for data holdings is to create a multi-level network system, building upon the existing structure. Such a system would give different levels of protection depending on the sensitivity of the data. At the lowest level of protection, that of public access, the primary security emphasis will be on availability and integrity. At the other end would be private or virtual private networks containing the most confidential information in the Agency's possession.

Summary

The security of information resources is very important to the EPA. We have taken and continue to take serious steps to address security risks, including many technological and process improvements. EPA has enhanced the understanding of managers and employees that information security is a critical component in fulfilling the Agency's mission. Perhaps even more importantly, EPA is working to see that all individuals accept personal responsibility and are held accountable for adhering to EPA's security policies.

GAO Contacts and Staff Acknowledgments

GAO Contact

Jean Boltz, (202) 512-6240

Acknowledgments

Other major contributors to this work were Nancy DeFrancesco, Michael Gilmore, Paula Moore, and William Wadsworth. In addition, the computer security test team provided significant support and included Gary Austin, Lon Chin, Debra Conner, Vernon Conyers, Edward Glagola, Harold Lewis, and Christopher Warweg.